SHARKMAN

A TRUE STORY

TOM VATER

To Lori
And to the sharks.

'Everything can and nothing must.'

— PETER HAUSER

SHARKMAN

ANDAMAN SEA, SOUTHERN THAILAND, 13/01/2022

PETER HAUSER IS A HAPPY MAN. He's lying in his hammock, a cold can of Leo in his right hand, a joint in his left, his lanky frame exhausted after spending the day floating above the coral reefs of the Koh Surin archipelago, his wry smile sliding a little closer to the sand as inebriation sets in. The tide is up, lapping at the powdery sand of Mai Ngam Bay, almost reaching up to his tent at the edge of the jungle. There's phosphorescence in the water, silver glitter cresting the low waves. Giant fruit bats circle overhead. Lizards scuttle in the undergrowth. Out, beyond the waves, the house reef is teeming with silent life. And death.

Ever since he was a teenager, Peter has been getting *Fernweh*, something akin to and yet more than wanderlust, the longing to be elsewhere. Most winters, he heads out to Thailand, to Koh Surin, to Mai Ngam Bay, where he spends three months, sleeping on a thin mattress in a small tent, fronting evergreen forest, facing the ocean. This three-hundred-metre sand crescent is framed by two sheer hillsides covered in dense rainforest. Eagles take off and land in the dense canopy. The vibe is almost pre-historic. Mai Ngam Bay is in Moo Ko Surin Marine National Park, a special, far corner of the world, home to sea nomads and an astounding variety of ocean life.

Peter doesn't come to Thailand to go sight-seeing, to get a tan or to find a girlfriend. Peter is here to swim with sharks. Out in the blue of the Andaman Sea, the truly fearless, or the truly mad, snorkel with tiger sharks, apex predators more than four metres long, that patrol the channels between the national park's jungle-covered islands.

Peter, tall, broad-shouldered and gangly, blessed with George Clooney movie star looks, more lust for life than Iggy Pop and a disarming smile, laughs at his fortitude, "It's amazing that after what I've experienced in life, everything still works in such a way that I can go swimming with these beautiful animals."

Peter lives in Kirchheim-Teck, a small town in south-west Germany. He's been working as a mechanic for Daimler Benz since he was sixteen. Growing up on a housing estate in even smaller-town Wernau, shirking military service, smoking dope, and listening to punk rock, Peter was always one for whom 'normal' life wasn't enough, one who wanted to learn something about his limits, one who wanted to see the world, wanted to talk to people. As if he'd escaped from the pages of the Brothers Grimm, he was 'the youth who went forth to learn what fear was'.

Peter learned a little more than he'd bargained for.

"It all kicked off exactly thirty years ago today. I was 28 years old. It was my sister's birthday. And my niece's birthday too, as I found out later. Just thinking about it now makes my hair stand on end. Africa!"

~

Peter, Klaus and Hummi arrived in Bordj Badji Mokhtar, a town of 16,000 souls - the last large settlement before the Algeria - Mali border, on the evening of **January 11ᵗʰ, 1992**.

The three friends drove battered Peugeot 504s. Peter had a Familial with three rows of seats. Klaus piloted a beautiful golden estate, while Hummi drove an ordinary model. The 504s, solid and strong cars, worked well in the desert.

"These cars were cheap. I paid a thousand marks for mine. They only had value in Africa. Most of these Peugeots became bush taxis. In Togo, they turned old cars into miracles. They cut them up and riveted them back together to make one out of two."

A jeep sat by the side of the road on the edge of town, riddled with bullet holes. A small convoy of Italians had traveled along the same route a month earlier. They'd tried to flee bandits who had opened fire with a machine gun mounted on their jeep. One of the Italians had died. The shot-up car remained, a gloomy monument to bad luck.

As the German travelers entered the town, children threw stones at them.

They reached the town's campsite, which looked abandoned and unfriendly, at sunset. They met another group of travelers who had decided to turn around and drive all the way back to Morocco. Hummi too was getting cold feet. He told his friends that he didn't want to cross the border. Peter and Klaus were adamant. As far as they were concerned, there was no turning back.

"We had everything. We bought pallets of beer at Penny Mart. We had canned food. We had rice, noodles, and onions. We had milk, oatmeal, muesli, and coffee with us. We bought a large ham in Spain. Klaus had a pull-out gas cooker. Each car carried 200 liters of fuel and 120 liters of water. In addition, we carried spare parts and tools. And we had good Michelin maps. There was more on those than there is on Google Earth today.

We were well prepared. And I didn't want to drive back."

They cooked and had a few beers, Peter and Klaus talking at Hummi. Heading back to the alternative and presumably safer Hoggar Route was too far, they didn't have enough petrol. There was just enough fuel to get back to the Moroccan border, and what would they do there? They had sold almost all their clothes. Peter was determined to sell his car in Africa.

As they sat talking, a woman appeared out of the night, covered in yellow powder. Her hair stuck together like clay. Nobody on the campsite wanted to talk to her. Other campers told her to get lost. She looked ageless. Perhaps she had once been beautiful, but now she looked emaciated and sad. Peter and his friends didn't mind her and she sat down with them and started giggling to herself while stacking their spent beer cans on top of one another, knocking them over and starting all over again. They offered her food and drink. She refused.

Hummi told his friends that he'd prefer to sell the car in Germany.

"I told Hummi that the cars were worthless back home, and by now, no longer legal. Klaus and I were totally positive, and I knew the route. We buried some money in Bordj Badji Mokhtar, to have something to fall back on in an emergency. And if anything happened, we'd just step on the gas. We pressured Hummi into acceptance and went to sleep."

The mud-caked yellow woman returned early in the morning of **January 12th**, with three carnations in her hand. She gave the flowers to the three travelers. How had she managed to conjure up three carnations in the desert?

"The flower of death," Hummi remarked.

The woman left with a lopsided smile, whispering incantations to herself. Peter and his friends broke up camp and headed to the police station. The immigration officers demanded to see the money they had declared upon entry into Algeria and the cars' papers.

The border guards checked the cars' chassis numbers against their documents. A rhombus had been carved in front of the chassis numbers on all three cars. The immigration officers suggested that this looked like a zero. That zero wasn't on their papers. Despite their protests, the officers told the travelers that they would have to wait for the boss to pass judgement.

They waited all day.

The chief of immigration showed up as the sun set and decided, in barely a minute, that their papers were in order. He put the necessary stamps into their documents.

They were free to go.

Peter and his companions decided to head back to the campsite for another night's sleep, but the border guards insisted that now that they had their exit stamps, they needed to leave Algeria immediately.

Bordj Badji Mokhtar lies less than a hundred kilometres north of the border. They got into their cars and drove into the night. There was no formal border demarcation, no fence, no border post, nothing. A few kilometres into Mali, a giant white sign loomed by the side of the road which informed them that they'd entered the country. Half-buried coils of barbed wire left over from the French-Algerian war still littered the Sahara and were invisible after dark. They were too scared to continue.

On both sides of the sign, low plateaus rose from the desert. They made camp in the shadow of one of these knolls, parked their cars in a triangle and cooked dinner. Peter told Klaus and Hummi that it was his sister's birthday and that she was also heavily pregnant and was perhaps giving birth to his niece that night. Everyone was a little nervous and Klaus stashed his cash in a film box and put it under one of the wheels of his car. They had a few beers and went to sleep early, as they wanted to get going at the crack of dawn.

~

In the 1960s, young adventurers traveled from London to Kathmandu. The route became known as the hippie trail. These counter-culture pioneers, disillusioned with the burgeoning consumer lifestyle back home, traveled on shoestring budgets. They were hungry for self-realization, drugs and the exotic. Following the revolution in Iran and the resultant closure of the Asia overland route, the road from Europe through West Africa to Togo became the classic post-hippie road trip alternative of the 1980s. Hundreds of young Westerners drove old cars across the Sahara. Many made it all the way to Togo's capital Lomé where they sold what was left of their sunburnt, tormented vehicles. There were two routes, through Morocco to Algeria, and to Togo: The 1000-mile Tanezrouft route into Mali, and the shorter but more dangerous Hoggar route through Niger. The last leg of both routes, through Burkina Faso and into Togo was the same. The Hoggar route was known for bandit attacks and travelers drove in convoys with military protection. Peter and his friends chose the Tanezrouft route, which Peter knew. That route was said to still be negotiable by individual travelers.

Only the Tuareg, nomadic Berber tribesmen whose clans live across Algeria, Mali, Niger, Libya, Nigeria and Burkina Faso, survive in the desert. Legends trace the community back to Tin Hinan, a queen referred to as 'the mother of us all', who lived in the 4th century AD. They call themselves *Imuschag* (the free) or *Kel Tagelmust* (people of the veil) as their faces are always wrapped in blue indigo scarves.

Following the demise of the French colonies, the Tuareg's movements were curtailed by newly emerging nation states and there's been intermittent armed and bloody resistance against dominating governments ever since.

Tanezrouft, long known as the *Land of Thirst* by the Tuareg, is one of the most desolate, featureless parts of the Sahara, most of it located in Algeria. The first traverse by car succeeded in 1922. There's little vegetation. There are no landmarks. The arid, dry landscape is shaped by the wind. In the summer, temperatures rise to 52 degrees Celsius.

"The Tanezrouft route, from Béchar in Algeria via Reggane to Tessalit and Gao in Mali was like a highway. You sped through the desert. The track was very bad, partially covered with corrugated iron," Peter remembers. "You had to step on the gas so that your wheels would always land on the tips of the metal sheets. If you drove too slowly, the car would tear apart."

Peter had first driven across the Sahara in 1989. Back then, he'd managed to reach Togo, sold his car, and caught malaria. Undaunted, he embarked on a second journey a year later, but experienced a paralytic ileus in Mali, only to be abandoned by his travel companions in Burkina Faso. With the muscle contractions that were supposed to move food through his intestines paralyzed and his kidneys malfunctioning, he drove himself in a near coma to Lomé from where he was medevacked back to Germany.

This time, Peter hit the road with more reliable wayfarers and good friends. Klaus had grown up on the same housing estate. Together they'd built sleds in the winter and listened to Pink Floyd, high on acid, in the summer. Born in 1958, the then 34-year-old had been on the road, gotten burnt by drugs, spent time in jail, and eventually become a landscape gardener. Hummi, real name also Peter, born in 1966, then 26, was the youngest of the three travelers. He came from Wentlingen, another small Swabian town. Blue-eyed and handsome, Hummi had always been happy-go-lucky, keeping to the sunny side of life. Nothing bad had ever happened to Hummi. When he was a kid, Hummi loved trains, and he worked for Deutsche Bahn, the German railways.

~

In the middle of the night of the **13th of January**, around two o'clock, Peter woke to the sound of a car engine. He jumped up and called the others, 'Hey, someone's coming,' and slipped into his pants and picked up a thick length of cable. His friends weren't armed, why would they be? As he jumped up, a shadow rushed at him. He could just make out a man sliding across the hood of his car, pointing a gun. More men appeared, about twenty in all, wrapped in blue indigo scarves. They carried handguns, long knives, and Kalashnikovs. Hummi managed to get into his pants, but Klaus stood facing the men in his long johns. Resistance was futile. The bandits pulled the three young travelers about a little and loaded them onto the back of one of their machine-gun mounted jeeps.

Peter had a pretty good idea who their captors were. They had fallen into the hands of Tuareg. The desert tribes were rebelling against the Algerian and Mali military along the border. These men were at war.

"We thought they'd kill us right away. The hair on my arms still stands up when I think about it. Hummi, on the back of the jeep, said it over and over again, 'They're going to shoot us now'. And I told him, 'No, they just want our cars, they'll just take our things, then they'll leave. We're going to go home. We'll find a way out of this back into our lives again. We'll survive.'"

The bandits started poking around in their cars, grabbing stuff. As they started Hummi's car, *Because It's*

Raining Today by The Angry Samoans blasted into the night.

"Hummi was totally shaken. Klaus was a tough guy, but he also swallowed hard."

The bandits were nervous and continued to train their guns on their captives. Eventually, they started the cars and drove off. Peter and his friends had masked the front lights and their kidnappers drove Hummi's car into barbed wire and tore up one of the tires. They couldn't open the trunk of the car. They called Peter over. They were very hectic, shaking their weapons in his face. Peter popped the trunk and they changed the wheel in a flash, removed the cardboard from the lights and headed into the night.

"If we could have driven during the day, that would have been great. We would have made it through. They wouldn't have gotten us with their jeeps unless they had cut us off. With the Peugeots, you raced through the desert at 100, the jeeps drive at most 80. But they screwed us at the border. I'm sure we were set up."

It was freezing cold. Peter, Klaus, and Hummi were more or less in their underwear, terrified, huddled together on one of the jeeps. The bandits drove an hour and a half until they reached a sprawling camp. Peter counted at least forty heavily armed bandits, but it was dark and besides a handful of goat skin tents, it was hard to make out anything. Their captors told them to get off the jeep and crawl under a large carpet. They were told to lie still, not to look out, and to remain there all night. An armed man stood guard. There was no escape.

"We were so frightened, but eventually we all fell asleep, exhausted, unable to change our situation."

~

The three adventurers had left Kirchheim-Teck **on New Year's Eve 1991** and had driven straight through to southern Spain. On **January 2ⁿᵈ**, they crossed from Algeciras to Melilla, a Spanish enclave squeezed between the Mediterranean and Morocco.

"The border was crazy. Gangs of entrepreneurial Moroccan guys were telling us to give them our passports. The guy we gave the documents to wore a hat with a bobble on top, just like you would imagine. Hey, this was the Orient and everyone looked freaky. Then our passports were gone, but somehow everything worked out, we got our documents back and managed to cross the border."

The three companions pushed quickly through Morocco. They lacked insurance documents and wanted to move on. They drove through Nador and Berkane, the road paved all the way, towards Algeria. But they had to be careful. Huge potholes that could easily smash a car's axle yawned in the tired tarmac. And the vehicles were heavy. Aside from food supplies and alcohol, each car carried 200 liters of fuel and 120 liters of water.

"We drove at night and suddenly I thought, what's that on the road? I hit the brakes. A police checkpoint loomed out of the dark. I almost ran them over. They had very small lamps. They stood stock still, a couple of meters in front of my car. In Ahfir, just before the border to Algeria, we slept in our cars."

On **January 3ʳᵈ**, the three friends crossed into Algeria. That border closed in 1994, due to tensions between Algeria and Morocco, and has yet to reopen.

Alcohol always spilled across the tables of border checkpoints. Most of the time, the guards were happy to get a couple of cans of beer in return for the necessary stamps, but some demanded a bottle of whiskey before the three amigos, as Peter liked to call them, were allowed to carry on. The French had the biggest problems crossing - the former colonial presence threw a long shadow across the Sahara. Germans too were confronted with their history, but in a quite different manner.

"You had to show your papers and open the trunk at many spots along the way, especially at borders. Then they saw your beers. Alcohol is forbidden everywhere in the Sahara. We're allowed to drink, but they're not. Alcohol was the best currency. Everyone wanted some. We would hand out a few beers and the guards would start to talk about how great Hitler was and we tried to change the subject and drive off as quickly as possible. They had that obsession everywhere we traveled in Africa; it was terrible."

Peter, Klaus, and Hummi all listened to the same music. Hummi owned a huge vinyl collection and Peter and Klaus had rummaged through his records and cassettes all summer, just around the corner from their pub where Hummi also DJ'd - punk rock, indie, rock. Now, finally on the road, they were all happy. Hummi listened to his music at top volume, windows down. Klaus, who had long lost his driving license to the German police, was content to be able to drive again without fear of getting arrested. They followed the unpaved 7A, populated by herds of goats, towards Maghnia, with stunning views of Morocco in their rear-view mirrors, before heading along the N99 to Douar Ouled and then via the N22 and N6 to Tlemcen Naama, towards the desert.

~

At sunrise on **January 14th**, the Tuareg started Hummi's car again. *Because It's Raining Today* brought the three friends back to their nightmarish reality.

The kidnappers lifted the carpet and told the three travelers to get up. Some of their captors spoke French. Hummi could speak a little, he had learned that at school. Klaus could also speak a few words. They were told to get to their cars and make their breakfast. The Peugeots were placed in such a way that they couldn't be driven off. The three young Germans were never alone. They agreed to stick together. Somehow, they would get through this.

Their captors were devout Muslims. They completed their morning prayers, and then prayed again at noon. Some prayed in rows of three or four men. Others found their own private places. Peter, Klaus, and Hummi were always under guard. There was no running or driving away. In any case, they were in the middle of the Sahara. Beyond the camp lay only sand, heat, and death.

"We made a good breakfast, perhaps the best breakfast ever. I thought they would let us go. They had our cars. But it had also crossed my mind that releasing us might have been the biggest risk they could take. If we disappeared altogether, no one would come looking for the cars. We'd left Algeria, but we'd never officially entered Mali. The whole thing would have just fizzled out."

Peter had his mind on his camera and screwed his courage up to ask their captors if he could have it back. But they weren't interested and wanted to know where their money was. The three travelers handed their travelers checks over. The bandits couldn't find their cash. Peter carried his inside his belt. Hummi had sewn his emergency funds into his pants. The film box full of cash that Klaus had squeezed under the wheel of his car remained there, for the time being. But that's another story.

The Tuareg made no attempt to search their prisoners, though they demanded a silver bangle that Hummi wore around his wrist, a souvenir from his girlfriend. They tried to take it, but he fought back and finally, they let him keep it.

"They knew we had money. The Algerian border

police knew exactly how much we had with us. Their chief must have arranged the entire catastrophe with these guys, for his share, while his minions kept us at the border. It was all staged, I'm sure. But they didn't touch us. I started thinking, maybe this isn't so bad after all."

After breakfast, Peter asked for his camera again, but the Tuareg were nervous and pushed the three travelers into Peter's car, the Familial with the three rows of seats.

Two men armed with Kalashnikovs sat in the back. The three friends were told to sit in the middle row, next to the spare petrol cans. The youngest of the bandits was in the passenger seat. The oldest, the boss of the group, was driving.

They headed out into the desert.

They drove in silence through flat, unforgiving dust-scapes, a murderous, angry sun overhead. There are few places on earth hotter than the southern Sahara. It almost never rains. There are no rivers. Famines are common. There are few landmarks. Peter tried to keep an eye on the sun's journey, to have some idea of where they were going, but the kidnappers kept changing direction and he soon got lost.

The four men kept their heads wrapped in *tagelmust*, long, indigo-colored pieces of cloth that served both as turbans and veils to keep the dust at bay. Tuareg men only unwrapped their face coverings when they were with their families. They were known as blue men of the desert because the powerful dye seeped into the skin of the wearers. The bright indigo textiles should have made the men less threatening, but the fact that Peter never saw their faces was disconcerting.

The driver was a cool, quiet and resolute man. He wore dark glasses and was probably just a shade under fifty. He looked more assured and stronger than the others. His *tagelmust* was the darkest which, as Peter had read, suggested he was the wealthiest of the bandits. All four men seemed perpetually angry, but there was something in the driver's demeanor that the others didn't have. He knew something. He spoke the best French. He was the man in charge.

The boy next to the driver was 18 or 19. He passed his time by sticking his unloaded pistol in their faces, and pulling the trigger, again and again. He looked keen to let his companions know that he was ready to kill the travelers.

The two men on the back seat didn't speak and didn't move. They were both in their thirties. One of them had painted his toenails, the only distinguishing mark in their collective appearance.

Sitting in the car, speeding into the vast desert, Peter was no longer sure they'd be able to get away.

"I remember looking out and seeing a partially buried skeleton, ribs reaching out of the sand. I thought, shit, this is where they're going to kill us. It was pretty crazy in my head. I said to Klaus, 'Before they kill us, we'll use their spare gas canisters to blow us all up'. We were going mad."

Their captors kept going. As they drove further south, the landscape occasionally looked familiar to Peter, who'd driven the route towards Gao twice before. Around mid-day, he spotted smoke in the distance. He knew that had to be a village called Adjelhoc. He'd not been there, but he was quietly relieved to know where they were, somewhere in the Kidal region of eastern Mali. If they found a way to get away from their captors….

"How do we behave? We didn't want to sit there and cry. We wanted to somehow keep our pride. They let us smoke cigarettes, so we smoked in the car. We didn't talk much, it irritated them. The driver, the boss, was watching us in the mirror the entire time, all day long. That was important to us. We craved that eye contact, even as his sunglasses kept him at a distance. The boy next to him was playing around with his gun. I had the feeling that the driver was having an internal discussion about what to do with us. We needed to be part of that discussion. He was calculating the odds. Would he let us go or would he kill us? Were we worthy of living? We implored him with our thoughts and stares. The boy would have loved to have shot us immediately."

Every now and then they saw groups of nomads. The three amigos were told to stay in the car. One of the men stayed with them. The kidnappers drank tea and exchanged information with the nomads. It was the bush phone.

"We circumnavigated a few small towns. We stayed away from larger Tuareg encampments. Our kidnappers really didn't want too many people to know about their passengers."

Towards evening, the Tuareg got nervous. The Kalashnikovs behind Peter and his companions rose up.

"I thought the whole time, they'll let us go. I felt like we got out of the camp because they wanted to get the cars to safety and then either disassemble them or just sell them and make their money. But they'd let us go. I mean, what else is one going to think? Of course, the smartest thing to do was to kill us. The desert is infinite. We'd left and disappeared somewhere in the desert. There would have been no outcry. I don't think much would have happened in Germany either."

Peter's mind was in freefall, bouncing back and forth, between life and death. Between everything and nothing at all.

They drove until the sun started to drop towards the horizon. They left the main tracks and headed into the big nowhere for half an hour.

Eventually the driver stopped. He turned and motioned Peter, Klaus, and Hummi to get out of the car and line up in a row.

The old man handed each of them a cigarette.

He didn't turn off the car's engine, it spluttered along and seemed like the only noise for thousands of kilometres.

No one said a word.

"It was so grim. Unreal."

One of the men who'd been on the back seat remained in the car. His companion stepped up behind the driver. He pushed a magazine into his gun. Peter found it hard to breathe or to look at his friends.

"I thought, this moment doesn't exist, it really doesn't need to."

Hummi refused to smoke his cigarette. He stepped away from his companions and started walking in mad circles, oblivious to their tormentors. He kept talking to himself. 'I don't believe that, I don't believe that,' over and over again. He stopped interacting with the world. He was denying its very existence.

"Hummi was wearing his trousers, his combat boots and a coat. Nothing else. Unshaven, wide-eyed, with the desert dust in his hair, he looked like a character in a spaghetti western. He looked so damn beautiful. Even in those last moments, there were films running in my head. My brain was getting flooded by stream of consciousness overload. Sergio Leone and Hummi. Life was a movie, pure cinema. God, there was so much to think about."

Klaus, watching their captors, said, "I've had to experience so many terrible things in my life. I've escaped heroin. I've cheated death again and again and now it has to end like this, here in the middle of nowhere? I'll be killed for being a tourist?"

Peter, almost hypnotized by the barrel of the gun pointing at them, whispered to his companions, "Guys, when he fires the first shot, we'll run. I'm not going to die standing around. I'll zig-zag across the sand until he picks me off."

The existential face-off in the great nowhere stretched on and on.

"I was thinking about my family. I was acutely aware that it was my sister's birthday. Maybe she'd had a child that would never know what happened to her uncle."

The bandits looked determined, standing by the car, their postures resolute, their expressions hidden by the cotton obscuring their faces. They were handsome, frightening, and absurd.

Peter and Klaus smoked their cigarettes down to the bone and dropped them in the sand. Dust devils rose and breezed past. The sunset was beautiful. They stood in near-silence, every breath underpinned by the car engine's intermittent purr. Hummi's mumbling, almost in time with the coughing engine, lay over the entire scene like a suffocating blanket.

Klaus shouted in bad French, 'You are bandits and we are tourists, that's no reason to kill us.'

To finance their journey, Peter, Klaus and Hummi sold clothes along the way. Many Algerians wore clothes from the GDR. The superior second-hand West German jumpers and pants the three amigos had in their vehicles were a hit. Petrol was scarce in the desert and gas stations would only sell the precious stuff if the three travelers opened up shop. The second-hand West German jumpers and pants were a hit. As Peter and his friends hadn't declared what they'd brought into the country, the impromptu bazaars were illegal and highly profitable.

"We were standing behind a petrol station in northern Algeria and a police car pulled up. We thought, that's it, we're going to get busted. But the gas station owner said, 'No problem, he just wants to shop.' We opened up our cars and pulled out fur hats, jackets, trousers. We were able to buy fuel for two cars. But there were so many hands in the cars that we got scared. A boy crawled deep into my car and grabbed what he could. I kicked his butt. Unfortunately, his father was the police chief. I gave papa a lamp and everything was ok. But I told the others, 'We're going to close up shop. We have our fuel, let's go.' They followed us in a column of taxis and waved wads of money out of the windows at us. But we lost them and headed on a gravel road into the mountains. As soon we stopped, other people came out of the bushes. We opened the shop again."

On the road to <u>Béchar</u>, they stopped in a village and went for a walk. When they came back, the cars were surrounded by children and Klaus' sunglasses were gone. He didn't see well with his left eye and he couldn't drive without them. Peter caught one of the boys and took him to his father who claimed that his son never stole and invited them to dinner around a TV which showed an aquarium, in black and white. After dinner, Peter brought the glasses up again and made it clear that they really needed them back. After a while, the father left. He returned with the glasses. He'd found them outside, he said, someone had left them.

The further the three travelers ventured into the desert, the more the desert appeared to invade them. There's nothing like driving in the Sahara – part extreme sport, part battle of resources. They pulled tights over their air-filters and stopped to clean them again and again. They taped up the head lights. The cars diminished in value with every broken light.

Once the road stopped, the land was pretty flat and Peter put his foot down, driving at a hundred kilometres an hour for long stretches.

"Ahead you see interweaving tracks. You look for the best trail and you hope that you don't get into deep sand. It's best to avoid corrugated iron sheets as much as possible. You have to go full throttle on corrugated iron and always look for another track. You're in a lane like that and the metal is scratching the underside of the car. But if you let off the gas and don't downshift, you get stuck in the sand."

The road south to Béchar was terrible and led through wadis, enormous river beds, dry for the most part. Sometimes the cars drove into sand fields and got stuck.

"We drove with the windows open because of the dust that got in every time we hit a pothole. If you closed the windows, you couldn't see anything. We looked mad, wrapped in scarves. We drove with the music turned to the max, drinking beer. We were flying without a license."

There was a false sense of space in the desert. One imagined a flat expanse, but barely visible ledges sent their fully loaded cars flying. As the three drivers sat enveloped in dust, focused only on the route ahead - which had to be guessed at as often as not - they were oblivious to dangers coming from either side of their track.

"I saw deep sand ahead and went flat out, shifted down a gear, and pushed ahead flat out again to get through. I look to the left and see Klaus coming straight at me. That was a movie moment, pure cinema. I saw his eyes widening as he tore the car around, and bang, he raced past me into deep sand. Missed me by half a metre."

Once lost in sand fields, the cars got stuck.

"We all had metal sheets with us. We were well

equipped. These perforated sheets had been used to build runways for planes in World War II. We had two with them each. If we got stuck, we deflated the tires and shoveled the wheels free. Then we tried to dig some space out under the wheels to get the car out with the help of the metal sheets. This process had to be repeated again and again until the car was moving again. We only stopped when the car was on stable ground. Then we ran back to collect the sheets. I got stuck like this, three or four times, mainly in Algeria."

Cars come to Africa to suffer - the corrugated iron on the desert tracks, the potholes, the lift off, it's the seventh circle of automobile hell.

"The frame of my car snapped. I noticed it because the dust poured in differently. I stopped and bent the frame back into shape. We managed to get to Béchar and the local welders sorted it out."

Béchar was a mesmerizing experience, a desert town straight out of a fairy tale. The three adventurers lost themselves in the vast medina. The markets were full of saffron and spices. They bought spare car parts in the handful of shops that catered to the thin flow of passing travelers. They bargained for textiles, light cotton scarves they wrapped their heads in while driving.

"There were only men on the street, very rarely a woman who'd be completely veiled or wore a burqa and was surrounded by men, you didn't see anything. One had the feeling that a lot of men were gay, out of necessity. A lot of men were holding hands. That was different among the Tuareg. In their villages, the women had a presence."

The three friends didn't linger. They had planned to drive from Germany to Togo in three weeks.

"In Algeria, I always had intestinal problems. The sausages were delicious but you got the shits. I drove through the desert and every pothole tore up my stomach. Sometimes driving through deep sand, I thought I was about to shit my pants. But I didn't dare hit the brake. I let the car coast, stopped, opened the door, pants down... one black drop... I had something extreme, but we kept going."

On **January 5th**, they reached the town of Igli. They parked their cars and went to a bakery to buy bread. As they were queuing in the shop, they noticed there was a crowd of men, dressed in djellabas, hoods up, forming outside.

"We got quite scared because we had no idea why they were out there. We'd only just arrived. When we got back to our cars, they were surrounded by hooded zombies. As soon as we jumped in, they started throwing stones at us. Hummi's car wouldn't start. Klaus and I got out of our cars, leaving the engines running. We pushed Hummi's car as all these men were closing in. Lucky, he did manage to start his engine. As soon as Hummi's car was running, I jumped into mine and took off. We raced out of town, over a bridge across a deep valley and stopped on the far side. They didn't follow us. But we'd really panicked. Generally, people in Algeria were super friendly. There'd been a total disconnect."

The desert proper started beyond the town of Adra, which Peter and his friends reached on **January 7th**. Here, Peter knew a mechanic called Omar who changed the shock absorbers on the cars and did a last check. They stayed in Adras's best hotel. Alcohol, of course, was banned in the hotel's restaurant, so they asked the staff where they might be able to get a drink. The waiters told them to step out of the hotel, circumnavigate the building and find a hole in the ground at the back.

"We could drink legally for once, even if it was in a dingy basement, along with all the town's least reputable men."

A few days later, driving towards Reggane **on Jan-**

uary 9th, Peter spotted a black cloud in the distance. He slowed the car, but he didn't want to stop and get stuck in the sand. The black cloud was mobile and full of purpose, and it raced towards them.

Then everything went black.

In an orgy of collective hara-kiri, thousands upon thousands of giant locusts smashed like furies into Peter's windscreen. Afraid that they would crack the glass, he stopped. Seconds later, they were gone, but for the unfortunates who had died on the window. The three travelers watched the cloud carry on in search of something, anything, to eat.

They covered the desert tracks down to Bordj Badji Mokhtar, the last Algerian town before the border to Mali as quickly as possible. There was little traffic. The area they passed through had an air of neglect. No government was in charge here. They stopped whenever they saw someone along the way, to ask if it was safe to continue. They were always told that it wasn't a problem.

~

Nothing happened for another eternity. The three friends stood, in shock, the sun beating down on them like a harbinger of death, the gun barrels pointing at them promising nothing but the end.

Then the driver nodded towards the impossibly blue sky.

Their would-be executioner lowered his gun and slid the magazine out of the weapon.

The young man who'd been on the passenger seat emptied his empty gun into their direction and cackled.

The driver didn't say a word and never looked at them again. None of the men did. It was as if the travelers had stopped existing. As if they were dead.

The kidnappers got into the car without another word.

As they drove off in a cloud of dust, the driver threw Peter's cheap leather bag out of the car. Peter thought he heard laughter.

~

Within a couple of minutes, Peter's car, with their tormentors inside, had gone. Disappeared. They were alone. They hugged and kissed. They jumped up and down on the hot sand. They were alive. They hadn't been shot. They weren't seeping into the desert sand. They weren't dead. The mood was weirdly, quietly ecstatic. But Hummi was close to a complete breakdown. They really were in the middle of the Sahara, not a track or trail in sight, their cars gone, their adventure broken.

"I knew the mountains in the distance, about twenty kilometers away. I knew we wouldn't die in the sand. I said, 'Guys, over there are the mountains, we'll see village lights there later. I've never been there, but I've seen it on the map – it's called Adjelhoc. We have to go there. But we can't walk there in the sun.' All the villages in the desert were Tuareg. I was hoping that there would be good Tuareg in Adjelhoc."

They emptied the bag the kidnappers had thrown from the car. It contained Peter's sleeping bag, their passports, two travelers' checks, two cans of beer and a water cannister. They tried to make some shade by draping the sleeping bag across a bush of thorns. They drank the beers and some of the water. Peter knew they would only make the twenty or so kilometres in the dark. The sun, even as it was about to drop below the horizon, was still cruelly hot. He told his friends it would be nice to walk under a starry sky.

"I figured that the best route to take was try and return to the point where the kidnappers had left the route south. There's always a bit of traffic in the desert and they had only driven a few kilometres off the track, no more than ten kilometres. Once we got back there, I just wanted to follow the main route to the mountains."

They lay down exhausted in what little shade the sleeping bag provided and waited for darkness.

~

"I wasn't afraid that the kidnappers might come back. It was clear to me that we had survived. We would live on. That was our destiny. We had to reach the village. We could do this. I was sure that these guys had already decided not to kill us when we left their camp. That's why they gave us water. They wanted us to survive. It was illogical that they let us go, after driving around all day. Or perhaps as time had passed in the car, these men realized that killing us wasn't a good thing. Perhaps the situation developed like this, while we were together in the car all day."

Happy but numb, they lay on the cooling sand for a couple of hours, until Peter spotted a shadow in the distance - something shimmered in a cloud of sand. He jumped up, ripped off his T-shirt, and started waving wildly as he ran towards the apparition. There was still a little daylight, the sun was just dipping below the horizon, and he could soon make out a truck. The driver spotted the three travelers and changed direction towards them.

The truck was filled with Tuareg, at least twenty men. It was on the way to Adjelhoc. Hummi was afraid to get into the truck, but Peter and Klaus convinced him to climb in. Their fellow travelers were friendly. But the truck was an ancient, worn down vehicle – they could have walked the thirty kilometres to the village almost as quickly.

As they arrived, the entire population of Adjelhoc

turned out and stood around the three travelers, discussing the new arrivals.

A loud voice rose above the melee, in perfect German, 'Ja, ja, Afrika ist gefährlich.' Africa is dangerous.

A black man, dressed in a kaftan, a white kufi on his head, appeared out of the crowd.

His name, he told them, was Otto.

"Our saving angel had appeared. When we met him, I knew we were safe."

The three exhausted friends had to tell their story again. They were given a mud hut to sleep in. Klaus told the villagers that they were traveling with two cars. He didn't want anyone to know he didn't have a driver's license.

"They kept asking us, wasn't it three cars? There was a shop that sold a few things. I went in there and saw a Tuareg with a painted toenail. I recognized the toenail. He was one of our kidnappers. I looked at him. He looked at me and I thought, now I'll shut up and pretend I don't know him. He looked at me closely, but I didn't say anything. I did tell Klaus and Hummi that some of these bandits lived in the village we had fled to. But I was sure that nothing more would happen. The villagers knew something had gone wrong. Maybe not the whole story, but the desert phones, they go fast."

In the evening, they ate with the villagers, a kind of goulash - rice with a red sauce and chunks of meat. It tasted awful. Their hosts scooped the broth onto their plates, chunks of meat so big that Peter could see the veins stick out. The hosts were happy to be hosts and they all ate together.

"I picked out a small piece of meat. Then I swallowed it. It was awful. I said that I was full and I put my chunks of meat on Klaus' plate. 'Oh Klaus, you must still be hungry'. Klaus had the decency to try to bite the chunks. I watched him chew through that. Hummi couldn't eat and said he was full. The sauce turned out to be goat's blood. That's what survival looked like."

~

It took Peter, Hummi, and Klaus another hair-raising eight days, until **January 22nd**, to reach Bamako, the capital of Mali. Hummi flew home on the first available plane, a week later. Peter and Klaus took several buses through Burkina Faso into Togo, all the way to Lomé, and then from there to Ghana to fly home.

"I thought even then, while we were still waiting for Hummi's plane in Bamako, that was just awesome that I was allowed to experience something like that. My life was already chaotic, and that had made it more so. But that was ok, I was at peace with myself very quickly. The only thing, was the bad conscience I had towards Hummi. We really pushed him. He kept saying, 'I'm going back, I don't want to'. We buried money before we got to the border in Bordj Badji Mokhtar. We told Hummi that if we came back, we'd have something. But in truth, we only did it to manipulate Hummi. At the time I thought, if we don't drive further, then I will set fire to my car right here. We had to move on. We couldn't turn back. Maybe the money is still there or someone peed on it and found it."

~

"The Africa experience gave Klaus a real boost. He moved into his trailer, which had a stove and a huge window, on the landscape gardening property. He planted a small field of cannabis plants. He later said, 'Boy, boy, that was a story.'"

Once he was out of Africa, Hummi understood that this was life.

"Nobody wants to experience something like that.

But if one got through it, it could be an enrichment. It's the same with all the stories I've experienced or survived in life. Those stories are what made me the person I am now, and help me knowing what's good for me and what I still want," Peter concludes.

None of the three adventurers returned to Africa.

Klaus died in a bicycle accident in 2003.

Peter and Hummi remain good friends.

~

Peter is fading in his hammock, breathing gently, in time with the incoming tide.

"My life is and was full. Getting to know people, other chaotic people, that was a privilege. Many are dead because they took it too far, in all directions - risk taking, drugs.

I enjoy life, every day. I have made up with my friends. Everything is fine with my ex-wife. You know how it is. 'Everything can and nothing has to'. I am happy that I can walk around this beautiful planet, and I hope it stays beautiful for a while longer. You have to remind yourself of that every day - we live on a small blue ball in a big universe. What a gift that everything fits so that we can exist, how beautiful is that? People look the other way and consume. And I'm lying here in my hammock. That's the way it is. Ultimately, we don't even know what's going to happen in two weeks. That's why I enjoy Surin. I am free here. The problems people carry around don't exist here."

As Peter finishes his last beer, his phone flashes.

'To our 2nd birthday. Best, Hummi.'

"It never goes away, but that's a good thing. It's my sister's birthday. It's my niece's birthday. It happened thirty years ago today, but Africa will always be out there, somewhere."

This morning Peter went snorkeling in Hing Kong, a

series of rocks that are part of the national park. The water is deep here and the current between the gigantic brown stones that rise up from the sandy seabed transports some swimmers out into the blue void of the Andaman Sea. Sharks, rays, dolphins, swordfish, and even whales pass by. But it's the sharks that have been calling Peter back to Koh Surin time and time again.

"The tiger was four meters long, it passed beneath me, made a circle and disappeared into the deep. I didn't swim after it, the visibility wasn't good. But it came back, and I dived down. I wanted to look straight in the eye of the tiger. I was looking into the eye of the Tuareg who let me live. I felt safe. I was at peace."

POSTSCRIPT

GETTING OUT OF AFRICA – AS TOLD BY PETER HAUSER

15/01/1992 ADJELHOC

WE HAD to stay in Adjelhoc for a while. The villagers gave us a baguette and a tube of mayonnaise every day, that was our food.

I still had my money and so did Hummi. Klaus was penniless, in his long underpants. But there were still 1,500 marks lying in the desert that Klaus had put under his tire. Maybe even 2000.

There were two cars in the village. We told Otto that there was money somewhere. His homeowner was one of the car owners. We then talked to that guy for a while. He was of course a Tuareg.

Hummi didn't feel like looking for the money. He was sure that we would be killed if we tried to go after it. He told us, "Leave the money, I'll give it to you when we get back home."

Me and Klaus said, "This money is somewhere in the desert, we can use it if we find it."

It was clear that Hummi wasn't interested. To him it looked like we were sliding into the next shit storm.

We decided to meet Otto, his house owner, and the village mufti to talk about the money.

Hummi was terrified that they would kill us if we

shared our secret, but the mufti was definitely a calming influence - a religious guy was involved in the negotiations.

We made a deal with Otto and the mufti and agreed on 50/50. What they did with their share of the money was their business. Everyone agreed that me and Klaus would go with two Tuareg. Hummi told us again, implored us, "We can't do that, they'll kill us in the desert for the shitty money. I'll pay you the money at home."

We couldn't leave him alone in Adjelhoc. He had been scared since we'd been kidnapped.

Klaus suggested to go alone. I would stay with Hummi. That was important, he was at the end of his nerves. I held him in my arms under the starry sky in the evening.

"Hummi, look at the sky, the stars, everything is beautiful. Everything will be fine. Klaus will be back tomorrow morning."

I'd already been in a few situations with him. We had once been on a bus in Peru at 5000 meters that had broken down. I knew him so well. That's why I stayed with him. We talked about life, and I kept telling him everything would be okay. I had to really talk to him. That he would be home soon. The villagers had told us that we would be picked up by the military. A Mali patrol came by every week. They passed through the area to try and combat the Tuareg rebellion.

16/01/1992 ADJELHOC

In the morning we made preparations for the trip and dressed Klaus up as a Tuareg. They set off around lunchtime, first to a village where they picked up a canister of goat's blood; then they stopped again and again when they saw nomads. I think it was 300 kilometers back to the border. They drove off into the evening but they didn't make it all the way back to the sign. They decided to camp in the desert and try to find Klaus' can at daylight the next morning. They made tea, cooked, and ate when another jeep came along. It was the same guys, the bandits, with the machine gun mounted on the car. The two guys from Adjelhoc told Klaus to get under his covers and shut up, not an arm out, nothing, not a piece of skin.

"You are a sleeping, tired Tuareg and they should leave you alone."

They came to drink tea, according to tradition. Klaus was shivering under his blanket and thought, "That's crazy, now I have the bandits sitting right in front of me. If they find out that I'm lying here..."

But at some point he fell asleep.

01/17/1992 ADJELHOC

When Klaus woke up in the morning, the bandits had gone. They got in the car, drove to our rest stop under the sign, got entangled in barbed wire and had a flat tire, just like the kidnappers. They found the 2000 marks, drove back without incident and were back in Adjelhoc by lunchtime. Hummi was a bit happier. We then divided the Marks Francs and Sefa into three piles. Everyone was happy.

In the following days, we walked around the village. For most of our trip we had only seen men, but the Tuareg women were out and about from time to time. They were more open than the Muslims we met in Algeria. They weren't so wrapped up and they were beautiful..

We were happy to have our mayonnaise with a can of fish and our baguettes, we got by on that because we weren't keen on the goulash. Hummi spent most of the time in the clay hut. He just didn't want to go out. We couldn't leave the village. People kept telling us it was dangerous; we would be picked up by the military.

The people in Adjelhoc were very friendly, really nice people who had nothing themselves and gave us what they could. In the evenings, they set up an old television and half the village came to watch. The guy whose house we lived in asked us to bring a big screen the next time we visited. Of course, we never brought the television. The situation slowly eased a bit and Hummi started coming out of his shell. We were able to give him a certain feeling of safety, because we had a good relationship with the important people in the village, the mufti and Otto.

01/20/1992 TO KIDAL

I had the impression that the soldiers knew that we were in the village. They came one morning in an old Russian tank and an old truck fully loaded with coal.

We said goodbye to the villagers. Otto's home-owner was a great man, and he took a risk for us and himself with the jeep. A few people were already sitting on the coal truck and we were told to join them. The Mali troops were not particularly friendly, but they wanted to hear our story. Klaus and Hummi went on strike. They had no desire to live through the past days again.

We set off around 9 a.m. into the blazing day. At midday, the heat was debilitating. We were all sweating like crazy. We drove through ravines where I thought an attack could come at any time. The soldiers always kept the machine guns up. The armored tank broke down. They repaired it. It continued for another ten kilometres, then something else broke. That was a day's torture, a real horror ride. We arrived in Kidal at sunset, we had managed barely 200 kilometers in ten hours. Kidal was a military post in the middle of the desert, not quite a fortress. They opened a prison cell for us and we spent the night there. They gave us a can of fish and baguette.

We tried to sleep, but the mosquitoes and the rats rustling in the cell didn't help.

01/21/1992 KIDAL TO GAO

The soldiers woke us up as the first rooster crowed at dawn. It was Klaus' birthday. They loaded us onto a jeep. Nobody explained anything. We drove out into the desert and eventually got to an airstrip. They left us there and told us that a plane was coming to take us to Bamako, the capital. Then they drove back to Kidal. And we stood in the middle of the desert. We had no water, nothing. A while later, a plane landed, an old Russian propeller plane, and I thought, OK, now we're finally getting out of here.

The pilot got out and was picked up in a jeep. Then people came on foot from the desert. They sat under the wings of the plane. I thought the pilot would definitely come back soon. But we sat there all day. Someone gave us some water and cigarettes. There was nothing else there, no building, nothing. Just desert. As the day went on, more and more people showed up.

When it was almost dark, the pilot returned. The plane was full, about half were civilians. We started straight away and I thought, now we're going to Bamako, finally. The guy next to me turned white; he was terrified of flying. But as soon as we were in the air we landed again, in Gao, a stopover.

Gao is a real city in the desert. We were picked up at the airport and driven straight to a police station. It was totally infested with mosquitoes. We had to tell our story again. Officially we had no cash, but somehow it became obvious that we still had two travel cheques. We asked the police officers where we could cash the cheques. Soon after, a guy showed up and took the cheques. We didn't even have to sign them. He gave us the money, 50US$ in Sefa. We went to a small disco with the police. The cops drank cola and we drank our first beers and celebrated Klaus' birthday. We were optimistic, happy. The next day we would continue to Bamako. Of course it was tough to tell the story over and over. The other two had really had enough.

1/22/1992 BAMAKO

At the crack of dawn we took the same plane to Bamako. At the airport we were taken to an incredibly fat guy who was sitting in a garden chair from which all the cords had already been torn out. He really hung in there. And he wanted to hear our story again. Klaus and Hummi refused at first, but that didn't work; they had to tell the guy everything before he put us in a car to the German embassy. The ambassador wasn't there and we were driven to his residence. He wasn't there either. This was the first time since the kidnapping I had been in a house. We looked… it was indescribable. We were still in the same clothes. Klaus wore his long underwear and Hummi was in his spaghetti western outfit. It was like a movie. When I looked into the bathroom mirror, I didn't recognize the guy who looked back at me. The ambassador's wife appeared and scurried around us dirtballs. She gave us a bit of money and we went to a market – we bought toothbrushes and underpants, a few other clothes. Klaus bought a large towel in blue and I bought one in red. Mine's hanging here, behind my tent, thirty years old.

The embassy took us to a hotel that we then had to pay for later. We called home and we somehow ordered money through Hummi's father. He also sent me and Klaus a little money. I called my parents, but my mother was in hospital and my father didn't understand what had happened. He didn't hear well. We had a flight home scheduled for Hummi towards the end of the month. But we couldn't afford the hotel until then and asked for alternatives.

We were taken to a youth hostel that had a room with a large bed and a mosquito net. You lay down under it and the outside of the net would turn black with mosquitoes. This was mosquito hell. We lay under the net and listened to the shrill screams of the insects. When we got out of bed and picked our clothes off a chair, a black cloud appeared in the room. There was a long hallway in front of our door. The toilet was at the end of the hallway. Next to it, a bunch of iguanas populated a wide area with rubbish and bushes during the day. In the evenings, they disappeared into a manhole. And the rats came out. They were white, like escaped lab rats, with crazy, long tails. Monster rats. We had to go through there every evening when we left the room.

When we arrived in Bamako it was clear to me that I didn't want to go home yet. I still had a month left. Klaus felt the same way. We told Hummi that we would stay with him until his flight left, but that we wouldn't come back to Germany with him. The days were tense because Hummi simply didn't want to be there anymore. Africa had gotten to him.

01/27/1992 HUMMI'S BIRTHDAY HAIRCUT

On his birthday, we took Hummi to a hairdresser in Bamako. There were hundreds of hairdressers, all Nigerian, who wanted to go to Europe and were stranded in Bamako. None of them wanted to go home.

The hairdresser started to cut Hummi's hair with his hand clippers. The thing was blunt and the guy ripped Hummi's hair out of his head. Hummi almost burst into tears. Klaus and I had a good laugh. When the hair was almost gone, the guy started scratching Hummi's head with a razor blade. Hummi really suffered and we started shouting at the hair dresser, it was so funny. That was terrible for him.

Bamako was a horror. There were riots during our stay and there were fires everywhere. Many, many people looked sick. But we wanted to get out to eat in the evenings. Hummi didn't want to come with us but we pulled him along. He refused on the night of his birthday, said he didn't want to go out the door anymore, didn't want to see all that shit anymore. Klaus and I went alone and drank a few beers. There was beer everywhere. That was not a problem in West Africa.

We gave a little money to a few beggars. Word got around and they waylaid us. We suddenly had a pack after us and had to run. That was brutal.

We saw a guy walking around with a sheep on his back, all day long. He kept coming over with the slaughtered animal over his shoulder. The next day it was a slightly different color. On the 4th day, it was green. He couldn't get rid of it. Then we didn't see him anymore.

Bamako is not a nice city. I don't want to go there again.

01/02/1992 LEAVING BAMAKO

In the end, Hummi was fine. We wished him all the best. He had a great girlfriend at home who would support him. He'd process our adventure and incorporate it into his life and he would be okay. He moved to Göttingen, got married and bought a house. He worked during the holidays and was enrolled in law school, but he never actually studied. Once he had processed everything, he came back to Kirchheim-Teck.

I still tell him that I'm sorry that I treated him like that back then. He was a good person but very soft. That was just an experience that really brought him down to earth. Life can be like that. But I think this life experience gave him a lot. He will confirm that to you. That's the case for me too. Hummi told me that it was amazing that we were able to experience a story like that.

Our case was taken up by the embassy. Otherwise we had nothing more to do with it. I seem to remember that Klaus told the ambassador that we had traveled in two cars. He was still worried that he wouldn't get his license back because he had driven halfway across Africa.

We left Bamako by bus on the same day that Hummi flew back to Germany. We had our passports. We wanted to get out of the city.

~

Peter and Klaus traveled through Burkina Faso to Togo where they stopped at the Abeposso camp site, a popular meeting place for Africa overlanders. From there they moved on Ghana and took a flight to Frankfurt via Moscow. They arrived back home in Kirchheim-Teck in early March 1992.

PASSING THROUGH THE EYE OF A NEEDLE – WAR IN THE SAHARA

PETER and his companions picked a terrible moment to cross from Algeria into Mali. While the route from Morrocco through Algeria into Mali and on to Burkina Faso had been relatively safe during Peter's two earlier attempts in 1989 and 1990, local politics and regional dynamics had changed significantly by the time the travelers arrived in the border town Bordj Badji Mokhtar in late 1991.

In northern Mali, a Tuareg rebellion against the government in Bamako was underway, while Algeria's military was about to annul parliamentary elections won by Islamist parties, which plunged the country into a brutal ten year civil conflict that cost between 44.000 and 200.000 lives.

THE TUAREG WAR

The Tuareg did not benefit a great deal from Mali's independence, following the departure of the French in 1960. Many tribesmen had expected that the vacuum left by the colonial power would lead to the creation of an independent Tuareg nation in northern Mali, southern Algeria and northern Niger. By 1962, tribesmen were attacking government posts in northern

Mali, but with the help of Morrocco and Algeria they were soon outgunned and routed by Mali's Soviet-armed military. By 1964, the rebellion was crushed and northern Mali was under military rule. Infrastructure programs promised by the government never materialized. Droughts in the 1970s and 1980s combined with overgrazing constricted the Tuareg way of life. Many young Tuareg fled to neighboring countries. In Libya, thousands received military training and absorbed Gadafi's revolutionary ideology. As these migrants returned, the government feared an independence movement and repressed the Tuareg all over again.

In March 1990, Mali's military government was removed in a coup which led to elections. But this changed little for the Tuareg and by mid-1990, a new insurgency was underway. Peter and his companions drove right into the heart of this volatile situation and fell victim to the lawlessness of the region. The government soon entered negotiations with the Tuareg and made promises of devolution and reform. By 1995, the violence had died down and many Tuareg had been absorbed into the Mali military. But reforms never materialized in northern Mali and Tuareg grievances continue to this day.

THE ALGERIAN CIVIL WAR

In late 1991, the unrest in northern Mali was compounded by the near-simultaneous collapse of democracy in neighboring Algeria. Since independence from the French in 1962, Algeria had been run by a single party government supported by the military. Municipal elections were held in 1990 and were won by Islamists. The same Islamic party overwhelmingly won the first round of parliamentary elections a year later, prompting a military coup.

Change through elections proved impossible. The

Islamic Party was dissolved and morphed into a fragmented guerilla movement that fought a brutal civil war against the government and parts of the country's population. Academics and intellectuals as well as foreigners were assassinated with terrible frequency while entire villages were massacred by increasingly radicalized Muslims, and perhaps, security forces.

In 1999, a newly elected president connected to the old military clique announced a blanket amnesty for Islamists and security forces. But despite the long shadow of the decade-long brutal civil war, true democratic reform remains elusive. In 2019, huge, peaceful demonstrations demanding reform once again rocked Algeria, but to no avail. The military class that wrested control of the country from the French remains ensconced in power to this day. Algerians are well aware that neither elections, peaceful demonstrations nor violent resistance change anything.

Voter turn-out for the 2021 election was 21%.

THE BIRTH OF SHARKMAN

THIS STORY IS DERIVED from 25 hours of interviews with Peter Hauser, recorded between shark encounters in Moo Koh Surin Marine National Park in Phangna Province, Thailand, from January to April 2022 and in Kirchheim-Teck, Germany, in August 2022.

ACKNOWLEDGMENTS

Eternal thanks to Peter Hauser for sharing his incredible life story.

My deepest appreciation for the Surin crew, some of whom have tolerated and intermittently embraced my sharkasm for years – Albert, Five, Kan (Plantongirl), Charlie, Mauro, Lori, Chom & Nut, Lena & Noah & Hook, M & Ben, Prisna, Willy Wysforce, Alva, Gore, Paulo, Apple (Pon), Abdul, Alek, Coco, Bodhi Garrett, Captain Tian, Tom & Am in Kuraburi, and the fabulously fearless Yumi Kajiwara.

A big shout-out goes to park rangers Nat and Kiem, and the Moken sea nomads of the Surin archipelago.

And to Irinia Flammetta Favaro, who provided a fascinating counterpoint to Peter's tale, to be published elsewhere.

Hats off to Richard S. Ehrlich, Carola Frentzen and Carlos Sardiña Galache for advice on the text.

Thanks to my agent Philip Patterson at Marjacq.

ABOUT THE AUTHOR

Tom Vater is a writer and editor working predominantly in Asia.

He has published six novels, including The Devil's Road to Kathmandu, and the Detective Maier trilogy.

His articles on Asian politics, tourism, the environment, minorities, and pop culture have been published in many publications including The Wall Street Journal, The Daily Telegraph, The Economist and Nikkei Asia.

To learn more about Tom Vater and discover more Next Chapter authors, visit our website at www.nextchapter.pub.

Sharkman
ISBN: 978-4-82419-335-3
Mass Market

Published by
Next Chapter
2-5-6 SANNO
SANNO BRIDGE
143-0023 Ota-Ku, Tokyo
+818035793528

14th April 2024

www.ingramcontent.com/pod-product-compliance
Lightning Source LLC
LaVergne TN
LVHW031241190726
843491LV00012B/3071